This Ginger book belongs to

_____

The Story of The Zodiac or Why Cats Chase Rats

Retold in English by Grace Bowman
Korean text by Kyoung Hye Lee
Illustrations by Sam Hyun Kim

This edition is published to be distributed in Great Britain only.

First published in hardback in South Korea by Yeowon Media Co., Ltd.
First published in paperback in Great Britain by Ginger Books in 2013

ISBN : 978-1-909642-08-9

Ginger Books is an imprint of Linco Press, a division of Linco Global Ltd.

Copyright © Yeowon Media Co., Ltd 2013

A CIP catalogue record for this title is available from the British Library.

Visit Ginger Books website at: www.gingerbooks.co.uk

Visit Yeowon Media Co., Ltd website at: www.tantani.com

Printed and bound in South Korea

The Story of the Zodiac

of the Zodiac

or

Why Cats Chase Rats

Kyoung Hye Lee | Grace Bowman

Illustrations by Sam Hyun Kim

Ginger Books

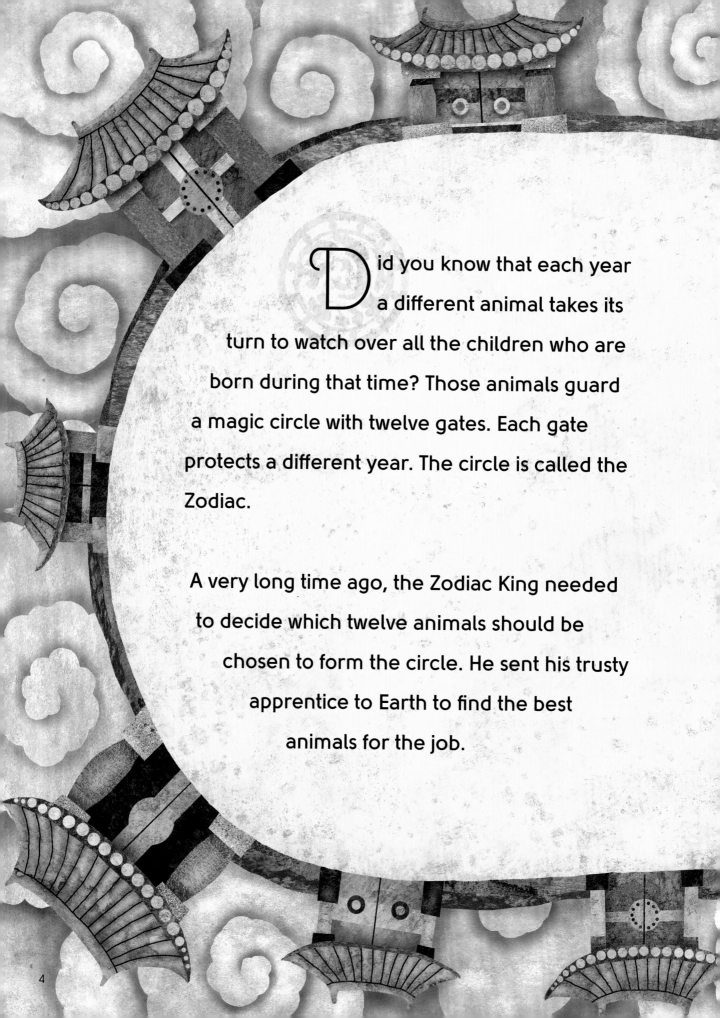

Did you know that each year a different animal takes its turn to watch over all the children who are born during that time? Those animals guard a magic circle with twelve gates. Each gate protects a different year. The circle is called the Zodiac.

A very long time ago, the Zodiac King needed to decide which twelve animals should be chosen to form the circle. He sent his trusty apprentice to Earth to find the best animals for the job.

When the apprentice arrived he was greeted by a cat. The cat jumped down from a high fence right in front of him. It landed lightly, skimming the ground. It jumped up again and pounced onto the fence. The apprentice was impressed by the fast and focused cat.

And so the cat was the first animal chosen for the circle.

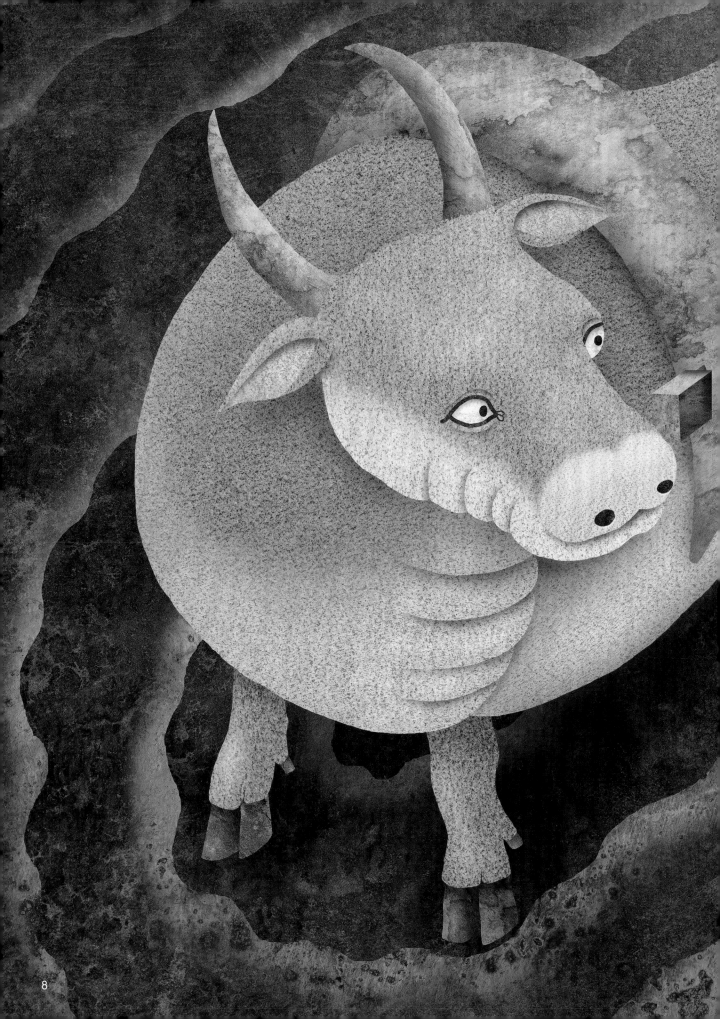

The apprentice moved on, walking through some muddy fields. There he saw a dependable, hard-working ox pulling a rake through the soil.

The apprentice was impressed and said to the ox, "You are strong and good at your work; you will be an excellent guardian!"

So the ox was the second to be chosen for the circle

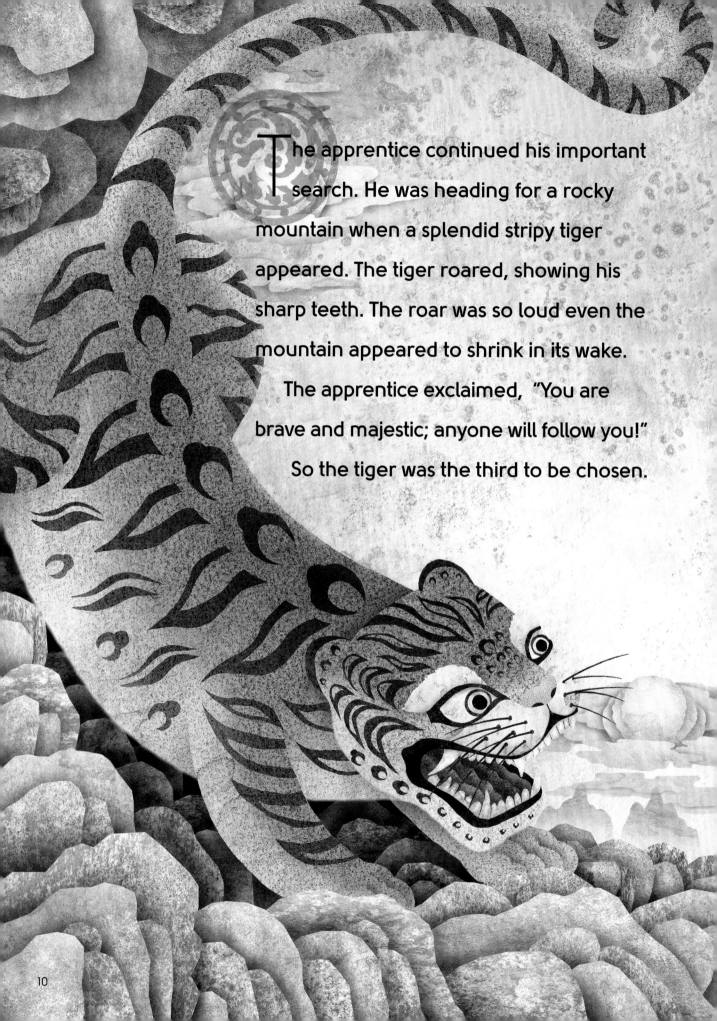

The apprentice continued his important search. He was heading for a rocky mountain when a splendid stripy tiger appeared. The tiger roared, showing his sharp teeth. The roar was so loud even the mountain appeared to shrink in its wake.

The apprentice exclaimed, "You are brave and majestic; anyone will follow you!"

So the tiger was the third to be chosen.

The apprentice was climbing up a steep hill, when a rabbit with two pointy ears sneaked out of the bushes and bounced up the hill with ease.

"You are nifty and nimble. You will be able to sense danger well," the apprentice explained.

So the rabbit was the fourth to be chosen.

As the apprentice continued, he crossed a lake. Suddenly, a dragon flew out of the water, whipping up a thunderstorm and showering rain down on top of him.

The apprentice was impressed. He said, "You have a magnificent talent. You will help water the dry soil!"

So the dragon became the fifth member of the circle.

When the apprentice looked up at the tree above him, there was a snake — fixed firmly — barely shaken by the storm.

The apprentice nodded with approval, "You are patient and tough."

And he chose the snake to join the circle as its sixth member.

The apprentice continued through a field, where a horse galloped towards him, making deep hoof prints in the land.

"You are a powerful runner," said the apprentice. "Whoever sees you gains courage from your strength."

So the horse became the seventh animal to be chosen.

The apprentice turned. He heard a sheep.
The sheep's soothing sounds were carried through the air.

The apprentice told him, "You bring peace amongst all the energy and action which surrounds us."

And so the apprentice chose the sheep as the eighth animal to join the circle.

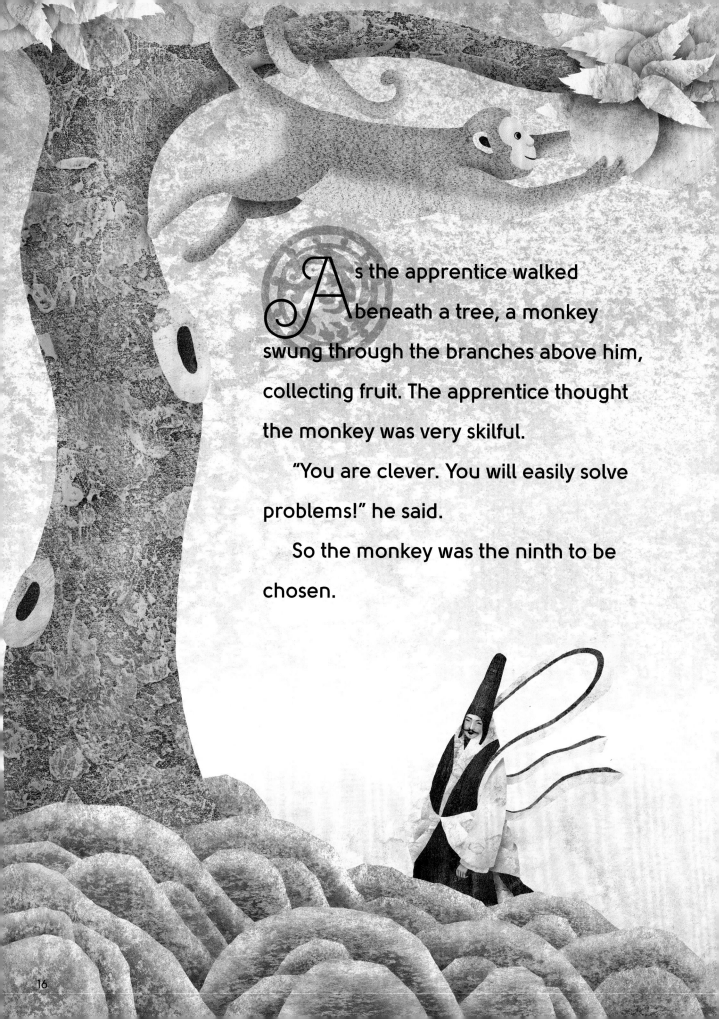

As the apprentice walked beneath a tree, a monkey swung through the branches above him, collecting fruit. The apprentice thought the monkey was very skilful.

"You are clever. You will easily solve problems!" he said.

So the monkey was the ninth to be chosen.

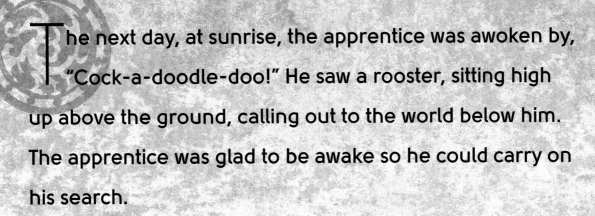

The next day, at sunrise, the apprentice was awoken by, "Cock-a-doodle-doo!" He saw a rooster, sitting high up above the ground, calling out to the world below him. The apprentice was glad to be awake so he could carry on his search.

He told the rooster, "You are diligent and you tell the right time. You will make everyone start the day early!"

So the rooster joined the Zodiac circle as the tenth animal.

As the apprentice began his walk, he approached a hut. A dog jumped out at him, panting loudly.

The apprentice saw that the dog was a good guard and told him, "You are trustful and reassuring."

And he chose the dog as the eleventh animal to join the circle.

The apprentice needed one more animal. He strolled by a field where a pig was munching quietly on his food. The pig seemed very relaxed and contented.

The apprentice said, "You eat everything and your body and heart are strong!"

So the pig was the twelfth animal.

He was the last to be chosen.

The apprentice gathered the twelve animals together. He told them, "You have been chosen as the most admirable animals on Earth. Because of your different skills, talents and strengths you will each become a guardian of the Zodiac. You will be a part of this great circle of animals."

The animals were pleased that the apprentice had noticed each one of them for their unique qualities.

As the apprentice spoke, a little rat nudged his head out of his hole, wrinkled up his nose and listened carefully. He was intrigued by what he heard and decided it would be fun to join in.

"I will follow them!" he said, and he tiptoed up to the ox, jumped as high as he could and grabbed on to its tail.

The apprentice took the animals up to the Zodiac in the sky. He didn't realise that he now had thirteen animals with him.

Once they arrived, the rat jumped down and hid himself among the white clouds. The apprentice told the animals to stand in line because the Zodiac King was about to arrive. And so they did: the cat, ox, tiger, rabbit, dragon, snake, horse, sheep, monkey, rooster, dog and the pig all lined up. The apprentice hoped his teacher would be happy with the selection.

The animals had to wait patiently. But the cat was distracted. Underneath a white cloud she saw something move — a little grey tail was peeping out. Her instinct told her to pounce but she didn't want to be seen, so she sneaked silently away to see what it was.

At that very moment the Zodiac King arrived. He was happy to see the animals, but was surprised. "Why are there are only eleven animals?" he said. The apprentice looked around anxiously. "There were definitely twelve animals here," he said, "I brought them here myself." He looked again and realised that the cat had gone.

The rat sensed the cat right behind him so he ran, leapt up and, quick as flash, presented himself in front of the Zodiac King.

"Hello," he said, "I'm the rat. Can I be of any assistance here? I notice you're an animal short and I'm always ready and eager to help."

The King thought for a moment. He saw that the rat was shrewd and willing.

"Cats always do their own thing," he said. "Is the cat a little too curious for her own good perhaps?" he muttered.

He turned to the rat. "I have made a decision," he said. "You will take the cat's place."

The rat was excited about his new role and scurried off into position.

When the cat returned she realised what had happened and she wasn't happy. She sprinted back to her place.

"Please," she purred, "let me re-join the circle. I can climb and jump and run better than a little rat."

But the King did not want to change things. He saw special qualities in the rat.

"Sorry," he said. "The rat took his opportunity at the right time. But listen to me; no one will forget that you were chosen. You are a guardian of the night. You will be ever-watchful with brilliant shining eyes."

So the twelve animals became guardians of the Zodiac. From the rat to the pig, each year a different animal takes its turn as leader and represents all the babies born in that year.

As for the cat, she never lost her curious streak.
As the King promised, she remained bright eyed
and alert, always on the lookout for clever little
rats and their tiny little tails.

Which Zodiac animal am I?

Rat
The Year of the Rat is a time of activity and renewal. It is a good time to make plans for the future. People born in the Rat Year are thought to be hardworking, witty, quick and shrewd.
Rat years: 1948, 1960, 1972, 1984, 1996, 2008

Ox
The Ox is a sign of wealth made through hard work. Those born in the Year of the Ox are thought to be patient, honest and hard-working.
Ox years: 1949, 1961, 1973, 1985, 1997, 2009

Tiger
The Year of the Tiger represents courage and gratitude. Tiger people are seen as sensitive, given to deep thinking and passion. Their bravery sometimes means they can be fiery!
Tiger years: 1950, 1962, 1974, 1986, 1998, 2010

Rabbit
The Rabbit is thought to be a lucky animal. It is sensitive and wise. Rabbit people often like their own space and like being quiet, but they also make good friends. They can be artistic too.
Rabbit years: 1951, 1963, 1975, 1987, 1999, 2011

Dragon
The Dragon is the mightiest of the signs. Dragons symbolise luck and power. Dragons are brave, positive and powerful and make good leaders. They frequently help others but rarely will they ask for help themselves.
Dragon years: 1952, 1964, 1976, 1988, 2000, 2012

Snake
People born in the Year of the Snake are keen and cunning, quite intelligent and wise. They are ambitious and like things to be perfect. The Year of the Snake represents prosperity and abundance.
Snake years: 1953, 1965, 1977, 1989, 2001, 2013

Horse
People born in the Year of the Horse are popular. They are thought of as cheerful and funny and they like entertainment and lots of people. They are very independent too.
Horse years: 1954, 1966, 1978, 1990, 2002, 2014

Sheep
People born in the Year of the Sheep are described as dependable, calm individuals, who are very creative and artistic. They can sometimes be a little shy or fearful.
Sheep years: 1955, 1967, 1979, 1991, 2003, 2015

Monkey
The Year of the Monkey represents talent. People born in the Year of the Monkey are said to be clever, skilful and inventive. They are sociable and have a positive nature.
Monkey years: 1956, 1968, 1980, 1992, 2004, 2016

Rooster
People born in the Year of the Rooster are said to be intelligent, shrewd, and sometimes stubborn when making decisions. It is said that in the Year of the Rooster, it is important to consider all the positives and negatives before making major decisions.
Rooster years: 1957, 1969, 1981, 1993, 2005, 2017

Dog
People born in the Year of the Dog are often very loyal, honest, bright and reassuring. They can sometimes be a bit defensive or stubborn. Dog people make good leaders.
Dog years: 1958, 1970, 1982, 1994, 2006, 2018

Pig
The last of the animal signs in the cycle is called the Year of the Pig (or Year of the Boar). People born in the Year of the Pig are said to be strong and honest. They are very loyal friends.
Pig years: 1959, 1971, 1983, 1995, 2007, 2019